HE WHO HATH AN EAR,
LET HIM HEAR

NORMAL LIFE PRETENDS
TO BE FOREVER. WHEN THE
NORMAL SENIOR CITIZEN
ABNORMALITIES TELL YOU
IT ISN'T SO, YOU START
DIGGING FOR LIGHT. FIRST
IN THE WOODPILE WITH AXE
& MALL, THEN IN THE EMPTY
STARING PAGES OF YOUR
NOTEBOOK WITH YOUR
    BALLPOINT PEN

SECRET LIGHT SURVIVAL IN
CATASTROPHIC CIRCUMSTANCES
— THE UNEXPECTED EMERGENCE
OF A HINT OF POSSIBLE LIGHT
WITHIN THE CATASTROPHY
ESCAPES THE HUMAN CAPACITY
TO ORGANIZE BUT MUST BE
UNDERSTOOD TO HELP US OUT
OF THE MESS

TO HELP YOU OUT OF THE
SLUMP, WE PROMISE TO NOT
STOP LOOKING TILL WE FIND
A CHUNK OF LIGHT THAT
CAN BE PACKED UP &
SENT TO YOU BY PARCEL POST

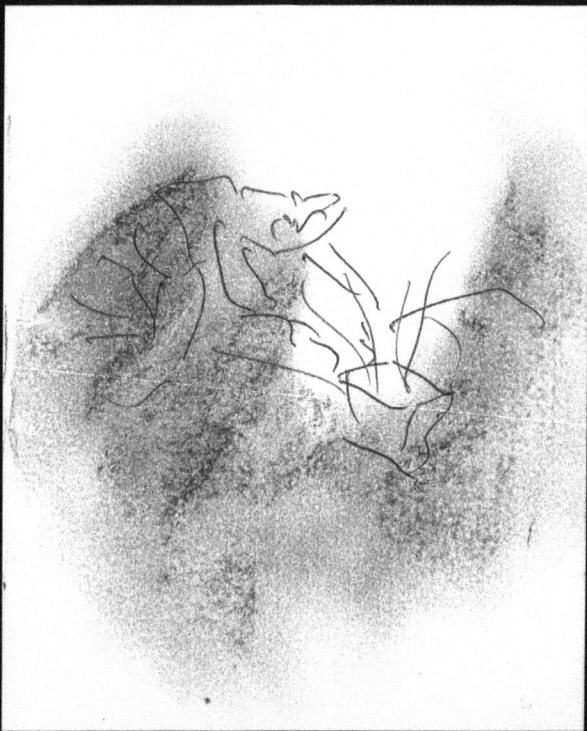

SUCCESS SEEKERS!
SUCCEEDING is SECONDARY
TO DISCOVERING THE LANDSCAPE
IN WHICH LIGHT HIDES
& CAN BE DUG UP &
BROUGHT HOME & MADE
        TO BLOOM

THE EVERYDAY OBSCURITIES
THAT COAT LIFE WITH LAYERS
OF IMPENETRABLE CURTAINS
OF DIFFICULTIES MUST BE
EXPOSED BY COURAGEOUS
HANDS THAT RIP THE CURTAIN
OFF THE DIFFICULTIES

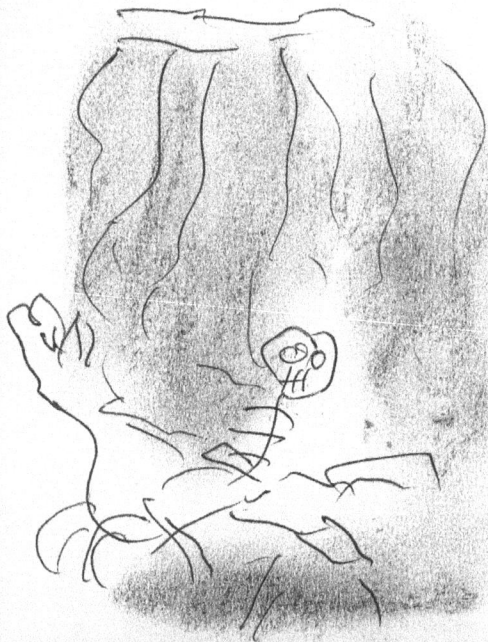

WE WHO SLOWLY GO UNDER
ARE NEVERTHESS INSPIRED
BY THE GLORIOUS SUNSET
THAT TEACHES GLORIOUS
EXITING

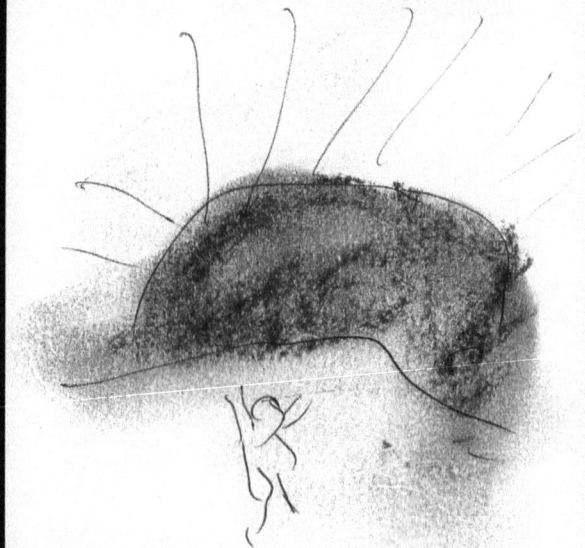

THE MOUSE i CAUGHT iN
THE TRAP & THREW IN THE
COMPOST BUCKET is AS
MINDBOGGLING BEAUTIFUL
AS THE SUNDOG WHICH
THE SUNRISE PRODUCED
THANKS TO THE iNDiSCRiMiNATE
LABOR OF LIGHT

THE WORKFORCE DROPS
ITS TOOLS, SINKS TO ITS
KNEES & RAISES ITS
ARMS TO PLEDGE
SUBMISSION TO ITS ONE
& ONLY BOSS : LIGHT

SCULPTORS ARE NEEDED
TO SCULPT ORDINARY
DAYLIGHT INTO THE
EXTRAORDINARY ICONS
THAT THE ALL REQUIRES
FROM US

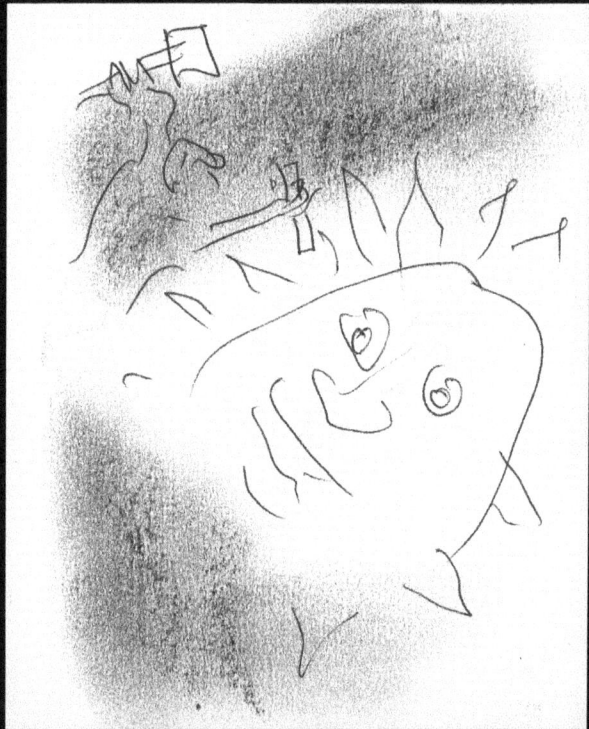

SWIMMING PAINFULLY
THROUGH ICECOLD
MORNING AIR —
THEN HIT OVER THE HEAD
BY SUNDOG MIRACLE
WHICH ACCOMPANIES
THE SUNRISE

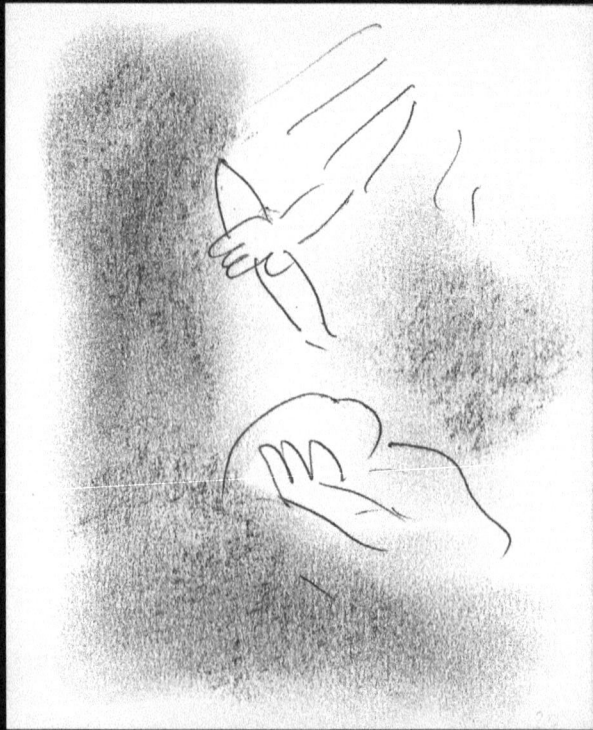

WHEN DEATH THREATENS
IN THE DISTANCE,
EMERGENCY SERVICES,
DESPAIRING OF THEIR
INEPTITUDE
PLEAD WITH HELIOS'
HORSES TO GET THEM
THERE QUICKLY

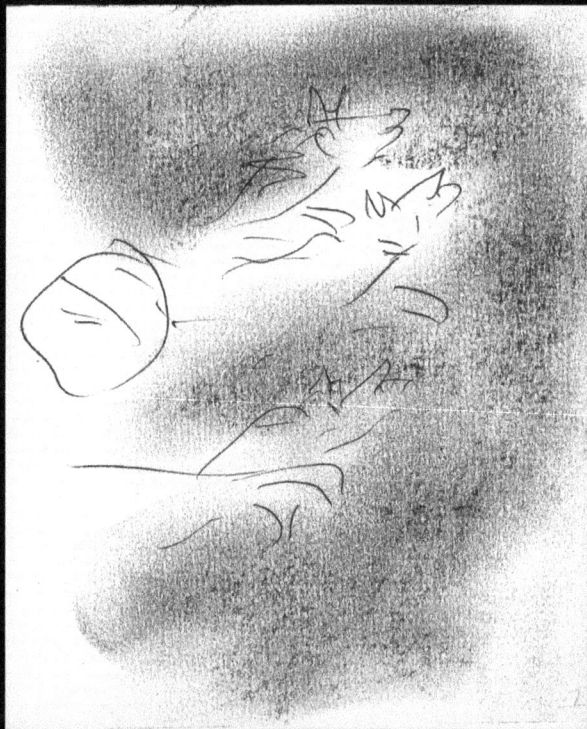

SUFFERING THROUGH
THOUSANDS OF MAN-MADE
DARKNESSES, LIGHT
DECIDES TO DECLARE
ITSELF

DECLARATION OF LIGHT

WHEN BABY LIGHT BECAME
A TODDLER, NOT YET ABLE TO
WALK FROM ONE SIDE OF
EXISTENCE TO THE OTHER,
IT INVENTED CRAWLING
& BY CRAWLING CAST
LIGHT INTO THE DARK
CORNERS

AGAIN & AGAIN NIMBLE
LIGHT CLIMBS TO THE TOP
OF THE MOUNTAIN & THEN
SPILLS ITS CONTENTS INTO
THE SUFFERING VALLEYS
BELOW

WHEN LIGHT DIGRESSED
FROM THE LOGICAL PATH
OF UNBRIDLED GROWTH &
PROGRESS, IT DID SO BY
REJOINING ITS ORIGINAL
HABITAT IN THE DEPTH
OF DARKNESS

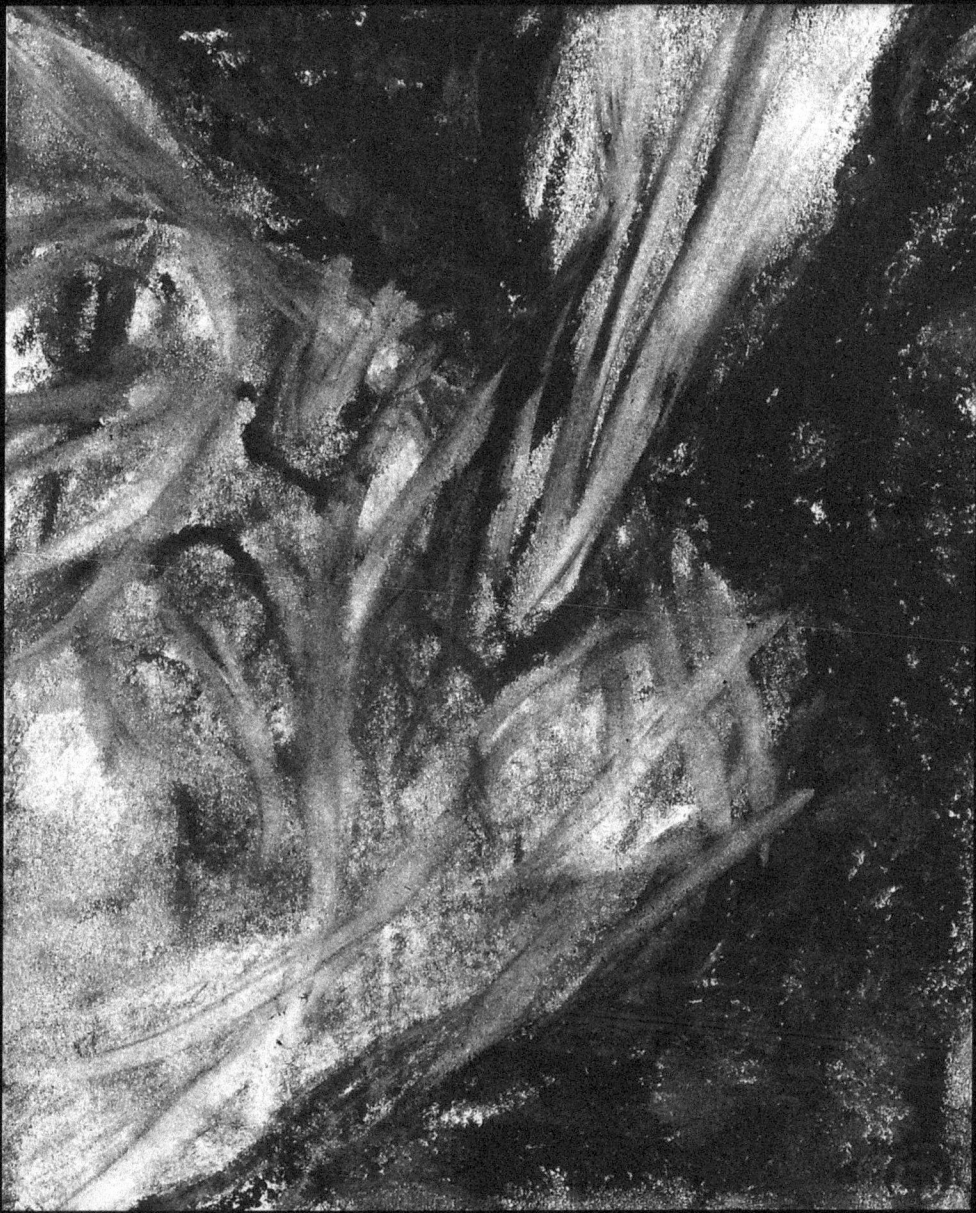

WHEN LIGHT RUSHED TO THE HELP OF THE TORTURED HUMANS, IT HAD TO ATTEMPT TO TEACH THEM THE SENSELESSNESS OF THEIR BRUTAL BEHAVIOR

WHEN LIGHT ALLOWED ITS
IMITATIONS TO PROLIFERATE
& TAKE OVER MOST OF ITS
DAILY FUNCTIONS, IT KNEW
IT WOULD SACRIFICE ITS
ORIGINAL MAJESTY & WAS
IN DANGER TO BECOME
ORDINARY & UNDERSTANDABLE

WHEN LIGHT DECIDED TO
LEND ITS SERVICE TO THE
HUMAN RACE, IT DID SO
TO GIVE HUMANS THEIR
YEARNING & SELF COMPREHENSION

SLEEPERS WHO ARE UNAWARE
OF THE INTENSE BATTLES WHICH
REALITY FIGHTS FOR ACCESS TO
THE BROOKS & RIVERS WHICH POUR
LIGHT FROM GREAT HEIGHTS INTO
THE LOWEST PLAINS & VALLEYS
ARE AWAKENED BY THE
THUNDEROUS ROAR WITH WHICH
LIGHT BREAKS THE ICE OF
THE FROZEN WORLD
— AND THEN HAVE TO RUSH
FORWARD TO PARTICIPATE IN THE
DISTRIBUTION OF WARMTH

WHEN TUNNELS ARE DUG TO
FORWARD HUMANITY FROM ONE
INHERITED DARKNESS TO THE NEXT,
THE GLIMMER OF LIGHT AT THE
END OF THE TUNNEL GIVES
THE WORKERS THE STRENGTH
TO CONTINUE & RAISES THE HOPE
FOR PROGRESSIVELY MORE LIGHT
AT THE END OF THE TUNNELS.
ONLY WHEN THE LAST TUNNEL
COLLAPSES AFTER THE GLORIOUS
ARRIVAL IN BRIGHT DAYLIGHT
WILL LIGHT ISSUE ITS VICTORY
DECLARATION

As winter darkens the
landscape, light occupies
the grey clouds & then
migrates in flocks like
birds from the above
to the below till the
earth is white

GREAT DARKNESS GROWS
  & GROWS TO BETTER
EMBRACE ITS RUMBUNCTIOUS
 CHILD LIGHT
TILL LIGHT BREAKS LOOSE
& ACTS ON ITS OWN BEHALF

MORNING HAPPENS
WHEN ENOUGH BIRDS
LOUDLY REQUEST THE
RISING SUN'S LIGHT
TILL DAY IS ACHIEVED

DECLARATION
OF LIGHT

PRE-EMINENCE OF STARRY SKY OVER
DRONE-INFESTED SMALL HUMAN EXISTENCE

EVERY RIDICULOUS MOMENT
OF OUR RIDICULOUS LIFE ASSUMES
IT CAN ASSESS THE SUM TOTAL
OF OUR PLANETARY EXISTENCE.
ONLY BY BEGGING THE BRIGHT
DAYLIGHT OUTSIDE OUR
KITCHEN WINDOW FOR ASSISTANCE
IN THE ASSESSMENT CAN WE
HOPE TO GET SOMEWHERE BETTER

QUO VADIS

MOTHER EARTH CENTRALITY IN BLOSSOMING
ENVIRONMENT AS REPORTED BY THE NY TIMES

ment receive

Payment sent to breada   betpre

Invoice ID: 100000341

        Go to the Help Center at: www.paypal.com/help.

Please do not   this email. This mailbox is not monitored and you will not rece
to your PayPal a   and click **Help** in the top right corner of any PayPal page.

You can receive pla   emails   d of HTML emails. To change your Notificati
go to your Profile, and   k My   ettings

UNHEARD-OF ILLUMINATIONS
SURPRISE THE EDUCATED THOUGHT
& THEN, JUST AS SURPRISINGLY
DECLINE & DROWN IN FASHIONABLE
IGNORANCE & STAY UNEXPLORED
& UNUSED TILL THE FULLY CAPABLE
FLASHLIGHT GETS INVENTED.
SPECIFICALLY DESIGNED TO
HIGHLIGHT THE MISSING
ENLIGHTENMENT

SUCCESSFUL MOTHER EARTH, THREATENED BY HEAVY DARK CLOUDS

HUMAN WORLD BLOWN APART BY TREMENDOUS WIND

PINK FOREST

AS THE ABSOLUTES FALL &
SHATTER THEIR PHYSICAL &
ETHEREAL BODIES, SCATTERING
ENDLESS DEBRIS OVER THE
ALREADY OVERLADEN PLANET
A SEVERE NEW STRAND OF
THE OBSCURE SPREADS QUICKLY,
SUFFOCATING ALL MINOR
DEVIATIONS OF LIGHT THAT STILL
EXIST — TILL COURAGE ARISES
FROM ONE UNIMPORTANT FRESH
LITTLE SPARK THAT REFUSES
TO BE SUFFOCATED & THEN
GROWS & SUCCEEDS

QUO VADIS

PAINED HUMANS CRAWLING & COLLAPSING
AS LIGHT & JOY ARISE AMIDST THEM

WORKFORCE BOOTS MARCHING ABOVE SISYPHUS'S SENSELESS LABOR

QUO VADIS

TREE'S SUNSET

RELEVANT AUTHORITIES, SUCH AS A DISEMBODIED KING
& THREE FRESHLY SAINTED BILLIONAIRE PHILANTHROPISTS
POINTING OUT SISYPHUS'S ETERNALLY SENSELESS LABOR

PROGRESS'S SEVEN ULTIMATE TEARS

HUMANIZED PLANET UNDER THE HOOVES OF UNKNOWN INVASION FORCE

TWO SUFFERERS IN STARRY SKY

INTERMISSION

UNDERNEATH LIGHT IS A
MOSTLY INVISIBLE LIGHT THAT
SERVES ILLEGAL ALIENS &
OTHER MINORITIES OF THE
HUMAN UNDERGROUND &
DERIVES ITS POWER FROM
ITS NECESSITY APPLYING
ITS DEVINE STRENGTH
WHERE IT IS MOST NEEDED

THE MORE-MORE-MORE BEHAVIOR
& ITS DESTRUCTIVE AFTERMATH
IS ASKED TO TURNON THE
NECESSARY LIGHTBULB THAT
WILL REVEAL TRUTH TO ITS
HABITS

CUSTOMERS OF LIGHT DON'T
NECESSARILY REALIZE THAT
THEIR LIFESPAN IS MEASURED
IN LIGHT ALLOCATIONS & GIFTS
WHICH ARE EXHAUSTIBLE &
EVENTUALLY EITHER ALLOWED
TO FADE AWAY OR DROP AWAY
ABRUPTLY

ELIMINATIONS OF LIGHT
OCCUR REGULARLY AS A
RESULT OF NATURE'S OR
HUMAN CRUELTIES &
REQUIRE ASSOCIATED
ENLIGHTENED THINKING
& DOING TO REPAIR THE
DAMAGE

GREAT ADVANCES IN
DARKNESS INVENTIONS ARE
CONTINUOUSLY PROVIDING
HUMANITY NEW FORMS OF
ANCIENT CHAOS IN WHICH
LIGHT RESIDES SECRETLY
& SHYLY & SEARCHES FOR
THE MIND'S POWERTOOLS TO
SMASH THE WALLS OF
DARKNESS

THINKERS DOING THEIR
THINKING IN OBSCURITY
EASILY CONSTRUCT A BRIGHT
UNIVERSE FROM THE BITSO
LIGHT OF A 60-WATT LIGHTBULB

THEREFORE

TREE OF LIGHT, SURROUNDED BY COWS & OTHER TROUBLED PLANETARIANS

ELSEWHERE

QUO VADIS

HERE

QUO QUO QUO

VADIS VADIS

VADIS

A CLOSE LOOK

Text within the artwork:

OBLIGATION:
THE UNFINISHED PLANET
OF YOUR THOUGHT

QUO VADIS

UNFINISHED PLANET

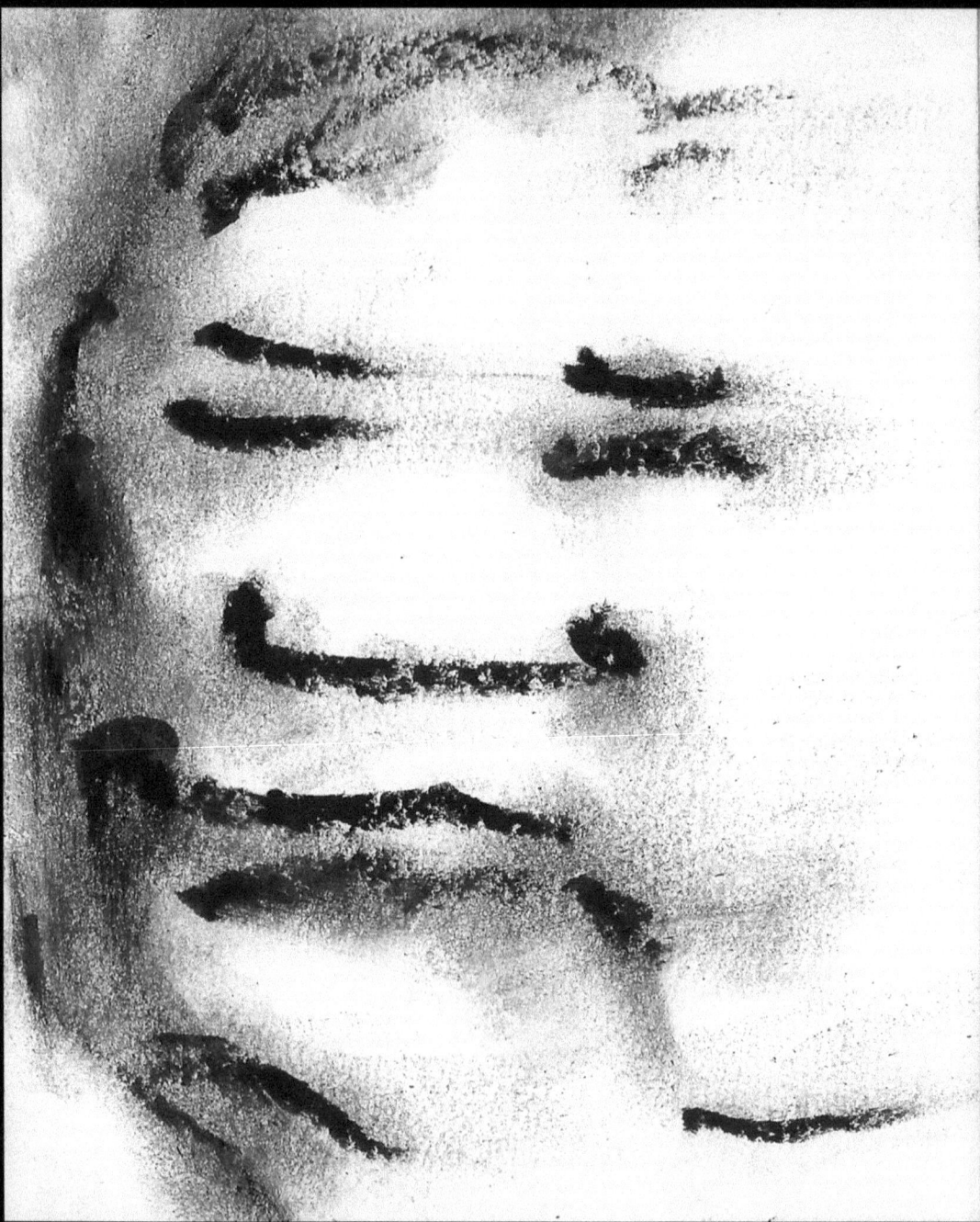

DANCERS DANCE ON THE WATER, CARS DRIVE OVER CLOUDS, HUMANS WITH CARDBOARD WINGS FLY THROUGH THE SKY WHEN THE REAL LIGHT HITS THEM

QUO VADIS

HERE IN THE PINK UNIVERSE YOU SEE EIGHT CITIZENS
TOTALLY UNAFFECTED BY THE HOLY COW PLANET

QUO VADIS

BUSY REDEFINING ITS
ESSENTIALS

THE LITTLE HUGE PLANET

THE MIND'S WEAPONRY

NONESSENTIALISTS

THE MIND'S SERVICES

DELIVER

SO MANY
NECESSARY
CHANGE

NECESSARY

HUMAN COCKROACH REBELLION

NECESSARY

QUO VADIS

INSURRECTION

LAMENTATION

RESURRECTION

SERVICES

PERTINENT SERVICES

APPLE HARVEST

POSSIBLE WINGS OF THE MASSES

QUO VADIS

TEASING DEATH AS THE HUMAN PLANET SPINS ON & ON

CHILD SURROUNDED BY GOOD SPIRITS,
BORN INTO CATASTROPHIC CIRCUMSTANCES

LANDSCAPE'S TORTURED INTERIOR

QUO VADIS

CIVILIZATION'S PLANETARY FENCE

LIGHTARMIES UNDER THE
COMMAND OF LIGHTGENERALS
HAVE TO ATTACK THE
MOST COMMON & THEREFORE
MOST UNRECOGNIZED
DARKNESS

EYELIDS, WINDOWS, DOORS
& CURTAINS MUST ALL
OPEN EXACTLY AT THE SAME
MOMENT OF TRUTH :
  THE ARRIVAL OF LIGHT

BABY HUMANITY ADDRESSES IMPRISONED PLANET

GREEN EMBRACE

BLUE EMBRACE

HOMAGE TO JASMILA ZBANIC FOR HER FILM "QUO VADIS, AIDA"

THESE REPURPOSED DISCARDED BEDSHEETS
& SCRAPS OF TORN SHEETS (DONATED BY
RICHARD BRIGHAM) WANT TO MITIGATE
PAIN & ENLIGHTEN DARK NIGHTS.
THE PAINT IS LATEX HOUSEPAINT
ACQUIRED AT LOCAL PAINTSALES BY
LINDA ELBOW. EXCERPTS FROM THE
PAINTED BEDSHEET COLLECTION ARE
REGULARLY EXHIBITED IN VERMONT
TOWNS BY ALEXIS SMITH. GARY
PATRICK HARVEY PHOTOGRAPHED THEM.
DONNA BISTER & MARC ESTRIN
CONCEIVED, EDITED & DESIGNED
THE BOOK.
THANK YOU ALL!
Re Schn

PETER SCHUMANN is the founder and director of the Bread & Puppet Theater. Born in Silesia, he was a sculptor and dancer in Germany before moving to the United States in 1961.

OTHER PETER SCHUMANN BOOKS FROM FOMITE

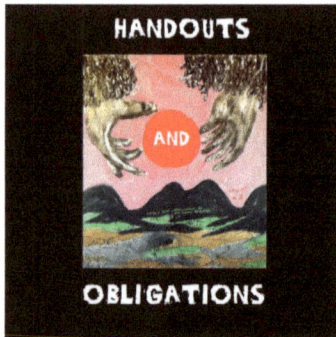

HANDOUTS AND OBLIGATIONS

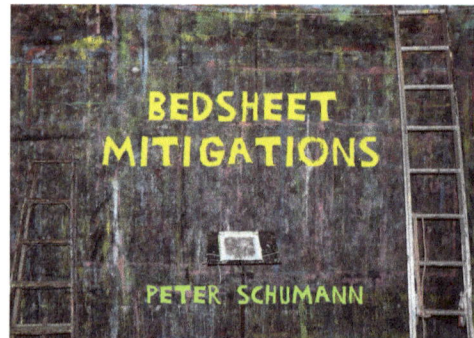

BEDSHEET MITIGATIONS

PETER SCHUMANN

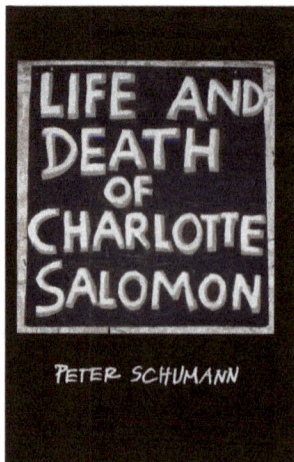

LIFE AND DEATH OF CHARLOTTE SALOMON

PETER SCHUMANN

FROM THE POSSIBILITARIAN ARSENAL OF BELLIGERENT & NOT SO BELLIGERENT SLOGANS

PETER SCHUMANN

PETER SCHUMANN

FAUST 3

Bread & Sentences

Peter Schumann

A CHILD'S DEPRIMER

BREAD + PUPPET

WE

PETER SCHUMANN

PLANET KASPER

PETER SCHUMANN

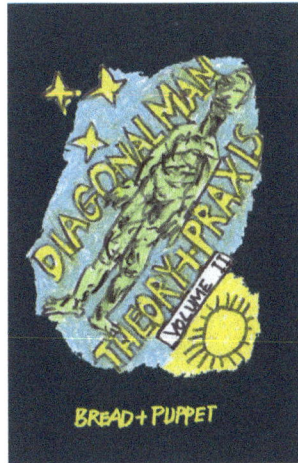

DIAGONAL MAN THEORY+PRAXIS

BREAD + PUPPET

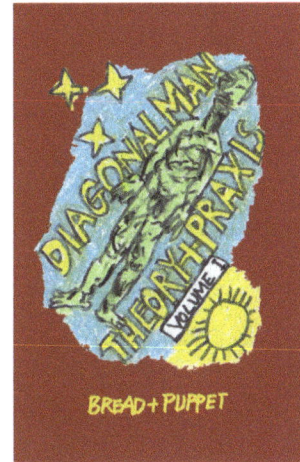

DIAGONAL MAN THEORY+PRAXIS

BREAD + PUPPET

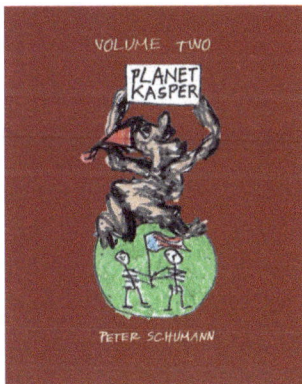

VOLUME TWO

PLANET KASPER

PETER SCHUMANN

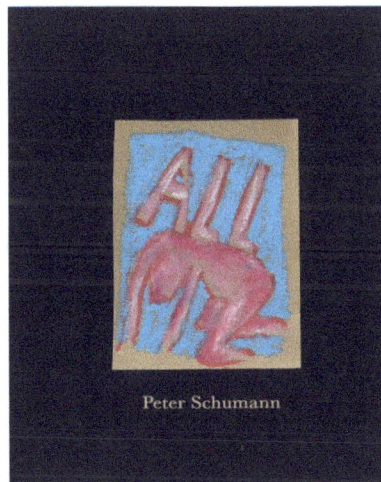

ALL

Peter Schumann

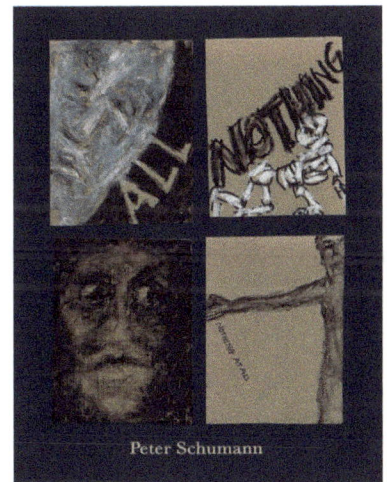

ALL NOTHING

Peter Schumann

ISBN-13: 978-1-953236-26-5
Library of Congress Number: 2021934682
4/1/2021